Let's Classify Organisms

by Kelli Hicks

Science Content Editor:
Shirley Duke

Educational Media

rourkeeducationalmedia.com

Teacher Notes available at
rem4teachers.com

Science Content Editor: Shirley Duke holds a bachelor's degree in biology and a master's degree in education from Austin College in Sherman, Texas. She taught science in Texas at all levels for twenty-five years before starting to write for children. Her science books include *You Can't Wear These Genes, Infections, Infestations, and Diseases, Enterprise STEM, Forces and Motion at Work, Environmental Disasters,* and *Gases.* She continues writing science books and also works as a science content editor.

www.rourkeeducationalmedia.com

Photo credits: Cover © Eric Gevaert, Serp, Kris Butler, foodonwhite, Sebastian Kaulitzki, Tumanyan; Table of Contents © Knorre; Page 4 © photonewman; Page 4/5 © Bjorn Stefanson; Page 6 © U.S. Fish and Wildlife Service, NASA, Sebastian Kaulitzki, dominique landau, Nicky Rhodes, Light & Magic Photography, worldswildlifewonders; Page 7 © Caitlin Mirra; Page 8 © Coprid; Page 9 © Sebastian Kaulitzki, Nicemonkey; Page 8/9 © Knorre, Wolframm Adlassnig; Page 10 © IgorGolovniov; Page 11 © worldswildlifewonders; Page 10/11 © dominique landau; Page 12 © Dariusz Majgier; Page 12/13 © Steve McWilliam; Page 14 © Dani Vincek; Page 15 © Nicky Rhodes; Page 14/15 © N. Frey Photography; Page 16 © Filipe B. Varela, artincamera; Page 17 © Alyssia Sheikh, Natursports; Page 18 © artincamera, Todd Boland, Light & Magic Photography, Audrey M Vasey, Sharon Day, irin-k; Page 19 © Alyssia Sheikh; Page 20 © Manda Nicholls, archana bhartia, Daryl H, D. Kucharski & K. Kucharska; Page 21 © davidpstephens, Kokhanchikov, Teze, frantisekhojdysz, Yuri Arcurs;

Editor: Jeanne Sturm

My Science Library series produced by Blue Door Publishing, Florida for Rourke Educational Media.

Library of Congress PCN Data

Hicks, Kelli.
Let's Classify Organisms / Kelli Kicks.
    p. cm. -- (My Science Library)
 ISBN 978-1-61810-098-6 (Hard cover) (alk. paper)
 ISBN 978-1-61810-231-7 (Soft cover)
Library of Congress Control Number: 2012930299

Rourke Educational Media
Printed in the United States of America,
North Mankato, Minnesota

rourkeeducationalmedia.com
customerservice@rourkeeducationalmedia.com
PO Box 643328 Vero Beach, Florida 32964

Table of Contents

Alike or Different?

Step outside and look all around. Do you see tall, leafy trees or brightly colored, sweet-smelling flowers? Maybe ants cross your path or you step in a puddle of water. Everything in our world can be grouped by similar **characteristics**. How would you classify the things you see?

All ants are classified as insects because they have three body segments, six legs, and a pair of antennae.

You may look at the colors or shape of an object to classify it, but scientists look at many other characteristics to group like objects together. They sort all living **organisms** into six kingdoms. Then they sort the six kingdoms into smaller groups based on how they are alike and how they are different.

Did You Know?

Scientists around the world use the same scientific words to describe organisms. While we might call an animal by its common name, scientists call it by its scientific name. The name is usually in Latin. A green sunfish is a *Lepomis cyanellus* to a scientist!

Kingdoms:

Archaebacteria

Eubacteria

Protista

Fungi

Plantae

Animalia

Two Kingdoms of Bacteria

Some organisms on our planet are very small. Many of these organisms consist of a small, simple cell with a **nucleus** not enclosed by a **membrane**. Scientists used to think all these organisms belonged in the same group, the kingdom Monera. Scientists have since discovered that there are striking differences that make it necessary to have two kingdoms of bacteria: archaebacteria and eubacteria, instead of one kingdom, Monera.

Archaebacteria like hot environments with no oxygen, and they produce their own food. Halobacteria belong in this group and they live in very hot, but also very salty places.

Archaebacteria thrive in the hot springs found in Yellowstone National Park.

Eubacteria make up the second kingdom. If you look at them under a microscope, you will see three different shapes of bacteria: cocci (round), bacilli (rod-shaped), and spirilli (spiral). Members of this group absorb food from their environment and some form chains, called mats.

Did You Know?

Some types of eubacteria cause diseases, but some types are beneficial to people, like the bacteria found in yogurt.

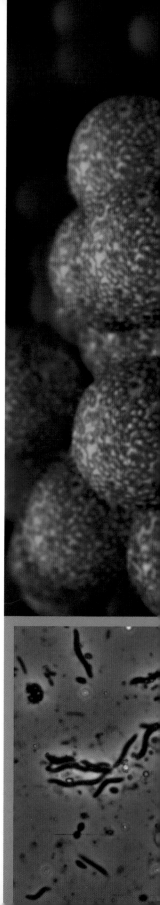

cocci bacteria

Scientists use a microscope to identify the three different shapes of bacteria.

spirilli bacteria

bacilli bacteria

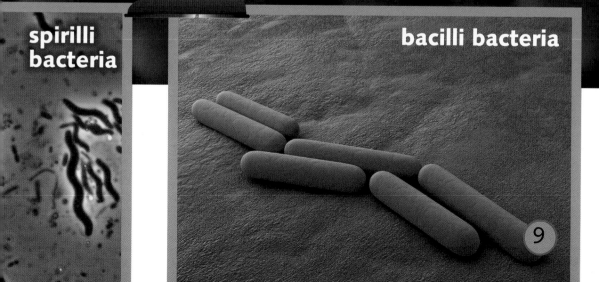

9

Kingdom Protista

Protista is a group of organisms with a nucleus enclosed by a membrane. Some gather in chains or **colonies**. Scientists sort the members of this kingdom into smaller groups based on how they move and how they absorb nutrients.

Amoebas are animal-like Protista and have cell material that slides in order to help them move. They surround their food and **ingest** it.

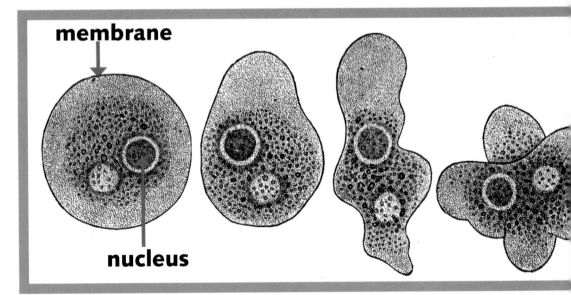

membrane

nucleus

Amoebas have flexible cell membranes and can change shape easily. Food particles float inside the cell membrane in a gooey substance called cytoplasm.

Many types of algae thrive in aquatic environments. They are an important link in the food chain.

Kelp and red, green, and brown algae are protists that are sometimes confused with plants. They produce their food like plants do. They have chlorophyll and make their own food to get nutrients. They are protists because they don't have the true plant cells. They are multi-celled, but their traits resemble other protists.

kelp

Some protists cannot make their own food. Instead, they absorb their food from the environment. They are **decomposers** like slime molds and water molds. That means they help objects to rot or decay in the environment.

insect egg
slime mold

This slime mold gets its name from its appearance.

orange slime mold

Kingdom Fungi

Many people with allergies have problems when they come into contact with the third kingdom, known as Fungi. These are multi-cellular organisms with cells that might be filamentous, or long and tubular, like the cells in bread mold. They have specialized **eukaryotic** cells and absorb nutrients from other organisms. Mold, mushrooms, yeast, and mildew all belong in this group.

Mold grows on bread when a fungal spore attaches to it. Mold grows best in a warm, moist environment.

Did You Know?

Many people eat mushrooms, a type of fungi. Unfortunately, some mushrooms are deadly when eaten. It is very difficult to identify which fungi are poisonous. Experts recommend only eating mushrooms that are purchased at a store or grown at home.

fly agaric mushrooms

honey mushrooms

Kingdom Plantae

Plants are organisms that don't need to look for nutrients. They are able to **photosynthesize**, or make their own food, with a little help from the Sun. When scientists break plants into smaller groups, they look at how the plants use water. **Vascular** plants can conduct water. Non-vascular plants need a moist environment because they don't have the ability to transport water.

Vascular plants have roots to absorb water and stems to conduct, or carry, water to the plant leaves.

Non-vascular plants, like moss, do not have roots and have to absorb water from their surrounding environment.

Did You Know?

The cell wall surrounds the plant cell, providing it with support and shape. The vacuole is a liquid-filled sac that also helps the cell keep its shape.

plant cell

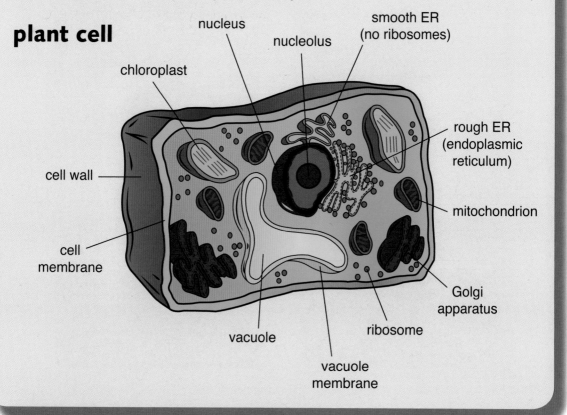

- nucleus
- nucleolus
- smooth ER (no ribosomes)
- chloroplast
- rough ER (endoplasmic reticulum)
- cell wall
- mitochondrion
- cell membrane
- Golgi apparatus
- vacuole
- ribosome
- vacuole membrane

Ferns have spores on the underside of their leaves.

spore

Scientists also group plants together if they have seeds, if they produce flowers, or if they have **spores**.

Kingdom Plantae:

Mosses

Liverworts

Ferns

Club Moss

Cone-bearing Plants

Flowering Plants

Kingdom Animalia

Animalia are multi-cellular organisms with specialized eukaryotic cells. They are the most complex organisms and have their own means of transportation. Not only do animals swallow their food, but they rely on other organisms for food.

animal cell

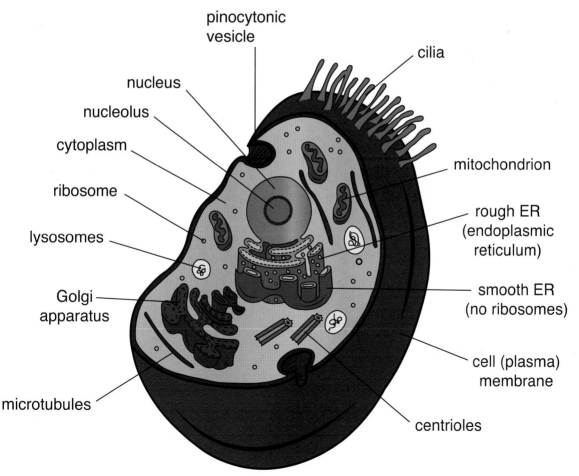

Compare the plant cell with the animal cell. How are the structures alike? What makes them different?

There are more than nine million species of animals on Earth. Humans belong to this group. By organizing groups of plants and animals, scientists are able to

Kingdom Animalia:

Porifera (Sponges) These are the saltwater sponges; there are approximately 8,000 separate species existing today.

Cnidaria This group is composed of jellyfish and other lower aquatic animals; approximately 15,000 species exist today.

Platyhelminthes These are the flatworms which inhabit both marine and freshwater habitats; over 15,000 species exist today.

Nematodes This **phylum** consists mainly of about 80,000 known parasitic worms.

Rotifers This group consists of about 1,800 highly-mobile freshwater invertebrate animals.

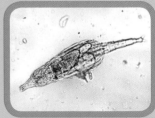

learn more about how organisms on Earth are connected and how they grow and change. What can you learn by classifying the creatures in our world?

Mollusca (Mollusks) This major group consists of snails, clams, squid, and octopus; there are over 110,000 known species.

Annelida (Segmented Worms) About 15,000 individual segmented worms comprise this phylum; the common earthworm is an example.

Arthropoda This very large group consists of insects; it is estimated that there are over 1 million species of insects existing today.

Echinodermata These are the marine starfish; about 6,000 species exist today.

Chordata This is a group of animals which are classified on the basis of possessing 3 common embryological features – dorsal nerve cord, supportive structure called the notocord, and pharyngeal gill pouches. Within this phylum is a highly-advanced group called the *vertebrates* which includes fish, amphibians, reptiles, birds, and mammals; it is this phylum to which humans belong.

Show What You Know

1. Which is the simplest Kingdom? Which is the most complex?

2. What characteristics are common for organisms in the Kingdom Plantae?

3. Which kingdoms contain single-celled organisms? Which contain multi-cellular organisms?

Glossary

characteristics (ka-rik-tuh-RISS-tiks): qualities or features

colonies (KOL-uh-neez): large groups of organisms that live together

decomposers (dee-kuhm-POZE-erz): organisms that contribute to the process of rotting or decaying

eukaryotic (u-kare-ee-AH-tic): having a nucleus surrounded by a membrane

ingest (in-JEST): to take food or some other substance into the body by swallowing or absorbing it

membrane (MEM-brayn): a thin layer of tissue or skin that covers an organ or cell

nucleus (NOO-klee-uhss): the central part of a cell

organisms (OR-guh-niz-uhmz): living plants or animals

photosynthesize (foh-toh-SIN-thuh-size): a chemical process where green plants make their own food

phylum (FILL-uhm): category that ranks above class and below kingdom

spores (SPORZ): plant cells, found on a plant that does not flower, that develop into a new plant

vascular (VAS-cue-lar): relating to carrying fluid

Index

Websites to Visit

www.kidsbiology.com

www.biology4kids.com

http://www.biologycorner.com/bio1/protista.html

About the Author

Kelli Hicks lives in Tampa with her two children Mackenzie and Barrett, her husband, and her golden retriever Gingerbread. She would classify her interests as sports, reading, and writing books for children.

 Ask The Author!
www.rem4students.com